CEO

CEO

----

by
GENE BROWN

Illustrated by
HENRY MARTIN

Produced by
Philip Lief and John Boswell

BANTAM BOOKS
TORONTO • NEW YORK • LONDON • SYDNEY • AUCKLAND

CEO

A Bantam Book/June 1984

Designed by Giorgetta Bell McRee

ISBN 0-553-34089-1

Published simultaneously in the United States and Canada

Bantam Books are published by Bantam Books, Inc. Its trademark, consisting of the words "Bantam Books" and the por-
trayal of a rooster, is registered in the United States Patent
and Trademark Office and in other countries. Marca Regis-
trada. Bantam Books, Inc., 666 Fifth Avenue, New York, New
York 10103.

PRINTED IN THE UNITED STATES OF AMERICA

CW   0 9 8 7 6 5 4 3 2 1

This book is dedicated to
Margaret Rose and Sylvia Tower,
friends in deed.

CEO

Graduation day at last! Five miserable years it's taken you to get there. While you toiled at the life insurance company processing Grim Reaper statistics during the day, you attended B-school classes at night. You took courses covering just about everything that can happen between the carefully calculated "good morning" and the totally insincere "good evening" of the typical business day. You studied business ethics with professors who might have frightened Captain Kidd and done gaming scenarios with students whose sporting instincts might have disposed them, given the opportunity, to throw a Christian or two to the lions.

But it was worth it; you've mastered business administration. You're an MBA. And you didn't give up five years of Sundays at the beach, weekday-night TV programs, and canasta games with your grandmother just so you could have a career as a middle-level junior muddlehead. You're going to shinny **all** the way up that greasy pole by hook or by crook. You're going to be Chief Executive Officer, and you're going to get there while you're still young enough to enjoy it.

So here you are at graduation listening to some old pompous ass carry on about how business is the fuel that makes this country run. **He** seems to run on a mixture of gas and hot air.

The three-martini lunch that your parents treat you to after the ceremony is a reminder that you now have to get down to the business of doing business. In the following weeks you go through one interview after another until you're finally able to cross your legs carefully and stare thoughtfully even in your sleep.

The company you settle on is traditionally structured — Marketing, Finance and Accounting, Product Development, Personnel, and Public Relations. Opportunity beckons in each division, but in each also lurks the pitfall of having to cross the paths of petty people who are thinking only of their own careers. You are not, after all, the only person like you out there.

An orientation meeting in DP reassures you though. The CEO lectures all the new MBAs about MBO, clarifies corporate MIS, and comes out strongly for the use of PERT. Whatever else is the case here, you now know that top management understands its acronyms.

The new MBAs and the old corporate war-horses lunch together the first day — a great opportunity for you to cultivate a mentor or two. But one thing is puzzling. You've been told all day that this corporation values individuality. So why is everyone wearing the same navy blue pinstripe suit?

The company is going to make a bold effort to increase market penetration among the over-85s. Since this group neither hears nor sees too well — and their memory is a little fuzzy — you wonder which media will be used to reach them. Perhaps Marketing plans a subliminal appeal to their latent sexuality.

You've barely gotten your wing tips wet and already a major decision looms. Should you help develop this product? Push it? Manage its production? Which is the fast track in this place? The success express is pulling out, and it behooves you not to end up in the caboose.

At this point, Bart Smith, market research VP, leans toward you, cups his hand to the side of his mouth, curls his lips slightly, and in a hoarse stage whisper intones, "In this company you're either a comer or a goner. I like the way you dialogue, kid. Be one of my boys, We have a multilateral, multidisciplinary, multiplicitous game plan."

3

If you think that Bart sounds like a corporate statesman — real chief executive material — and is a bright star for you to hitch your wagon to, turn to page 67.

If you think this Bart is a turkey trying unsuccessfully to speak English, turn to page 4.

You give it to Bart straight: "I'm afraid you guys are a bit too multilinear for me."

Unknown to you, you have just passed an important test of your critical judgment, and top management is very impressed. This Bart was an amateur actor hired to entrap smarty-pants MBAs. You managed to get the point without getting shafted.

But you still have to decide which division of the company you'll join. One old hand suggests that Finance and Accounting is the quickest route to the top. But while that may be the case, that's **toadyville** — you can expect to be eating humble pie with your martinis. Marketing is the creative end, advises another company old-timer. It's also the place with the perks: admittance to the corporate tennis club, accessories from the Mark Cross catalogue, a Golden Parachute in your future.

4

If you choose to take the slow but steady route and grope your way up into the executive suite by groveling in Finance and Accounting, turn to page 16.

But if you want to try your hand at the creative sell and your pulse quickens at the thought of those perks in Marketing, turn to page 10.

New product development has always been a problem for your company. The public tends to react not so much as if they were being sold convenience, shopping, or specialty goods, but rather a bill of goods. Retailers panic and begin to dump their inventory fire-sale fashion before they even get around to setting their insurance fires. Cynics among store-owners refer to your firm as "Burn, Baby, Burn & Co."

You join the product planning committee, which this time is determined to pick a winner. They decide to go geriatric. Here's your chance. You point out that false teeth are as staple an item for the over-85s as milk, bread, and cocaine are for their grandchildren. You suggest redefining the product to get rid of its negative image. "False teeth" sounds double-dealing, disingenuous. What's needed, you maintain, is a mildly ironic, laid-back, friendly, unthreatening name. Your suggestion of "Mock Teeth" is received with wild enthusiasm.

5

If you favor hiring an ad agency to build demand for this thing gradually, turn to page 24.

If you think that the company should keep it in-house and roll it all on one spectacular special promotion, turn to page 27.

Good choice! "Comptroller" originated as an erroneous spelling of "controller." At this company you can do or say almost anything as long as you spell it correctly.

With more time to look around, you realize that this is a strange place staffed by weird people. Gaunt, tight-lipped bookkeepers and accountants wearing eyeshades bend over dusty ledgers in the dim light, painstakingly entering their figures with quills dipped in ink, working late into the night, and speaking only when they are spoken to. They are not a lively group, and you do not look forward to their Christmas party.

Your choice of "controller" gets your promoted to assistant department head in charge of cash management. Your predecessor had peculiar ideas as to what constituted sound short-term investments. Much of the firm's loose cash was lent out on the street at 45 percent interest, compounded weekly. Some of it was in pork-belly futures, while a tidy sum was sunk into a national chain of escargot-to-go stands. But it was the grubstake he advanced to his brother-in-law for an antique shop–cum–pizzeria that appears to have been his undoing.

You quickly become master of the awesome audit and there is a pronounced lessening of legerdemain under your clinically ruthless regime. You are a young MBA on the move, but so far your star has yet to shine beyond the bottom line of the balance sheet. You need to meet new people and conquer new worlds.

If you now pick a laid-back pastoral path and opt for the company picnic as the rustic route to success — not to mention an opportunity for some splendor in the grass — turn to page 11.

If, on the other hand, you choose to stay aggressive with the aim of striking out in new directions and scoring a big hit with management by getting them to play ball your way, turn to page 13.

6

ANTONIO & PHYFE'S
Antiques 'n' Pizzas
SPECIALS
QUEEN ANNE HIGHBOY
PEPPERONI PIZZA
CHIPPENDALE CHAIR
MUSHROOM PIZZA
SHERATON TABLE
ANCHOVY PIZZA

7

Now that you know what you're up against, you decide that a factor evaluation of the group dynamics at the juncture at which social interaction intersects online with hydraulic flow might be indicated at this time. In other words, you head for the water cooler.

Mabel Moynihan, assistant vice-president for advertising once removed, has the same idea. She softly draws water from the tap and presses the lip of the cup sensuously against her own lips. You yank the knob, cascading water into your cup with a masculine force, and down its contents in one gulp, crushing the cup afterward in a prolonged squeeze. You eyeball her; she contemplates you.

"Horizontal combinations," she whispers.

"What?" you reply.

"Joint ventures, mergers," you think she says as she languidly sips from her cup.

What is she getting at? Feverishly you search your brain for the textbook memories that will tell you what she's talking about. Five years of business school and you draw a blank.

"You have a PERT demand curve," you finally venture somewhat tentatively.

She wheels and stalks back to her office, leaving you standing there bewildered. You are also dripping water on your shoes from the remains of your cup.

The **mot juste** just appears to be **de rigueur** here.

If your encounter with Moynihan convinces you that the cultivation of personal relationships takes priority at this place and that the pursuit of office politics is the arena in which the big prize may be won, turn to page 17.

On the other hand, if you decide to take the higher road, concentrate only on matters of substance, and improve the company's product mix by lending your considerable talents to product development, turn to page 5.

9

The perks are slow to appear. Nevertheless, you are still sure that Marketing is where the action is, and although any mistake you make in this department might prove to be your undoing, if you succeed here you could go right to the top.

In your first week you have to endure a little hostility from down in the ranks. They're still upset at the untimely departure of your predecessor. Some people never accepted it and hold out the hope that he is merely taking an exceptionally long lunch. He came to work one day to find his in-box empty, his outsized coatrack gone, his input no longer asked for, his output chart removed, and a notice from in-house job counseling to come down for an interview. In a word, he had been outplaced.

Your assistant, Bill Sneed, is a reptilian individual. When he speaks, he draws in his breath after each word, making a hissing sound. He greases his hair, and his black suit clings to him like a second skin; no doubt he sheds it periodically. He's the kind of person who can quickly empty a crowded elevator. You wouldn't touch him with a ten-foot pole, but you might be willing to approach him with a forked stick. Nevertheless, he's an asset to your department; he could probably sell snake oil to a snake.

- -

Turn to page 8.

Charles Evans Osgood, Choate '40, USMC, 1942–45, Princeton '47, the CEO of your company, hosts a mean picnic. All the activities are carefully scheduled. As a matter of fact, he's had Data Processing working full time critical-pathing the big event, beginning with a week before C hour, so called because of Osgood's infamous cucumber sandwiches, traditionally the main repast at these bacchanals.

Chartered buses take the happy lot of you out to Empty Hollow State Park. You proceed directly to your assigned blankets, laid out and numbered precisely according to Osgood's chart. Similarly numbered picnic hampers are carted in by the maintenance crew. Has Osgood, you wonder, also assigned stations to the ants?

No sooner are you settled than Snodgrass, who's still smarting from having been so wrong on "comptroller," is up, glad-handing his way from blanket to blanket, accumulating brownie points. Inevitably he oversteps, crosses the path used by the locals to walk their dogs, and steps in it.

You're not above doing your own politicking. You hang around the personnel blankets for a while, acting as personable as you can, and do a quick-sale of yourself to the Marketing people camped nearby. You even make some luncheon dates and set up some possible bridge foursomes. Sylvester Titeseet invites you to play cards with him. He's the guy who writes out the pink slips in a beautiful calligraphy. "The Turk," as he is called, wants to play hearts, but you're seeking bigger game and pass up the pleasure.

Cucumber sandwiches be damned, you want the big enchilada: Osgood. He and the other big boys are seated on a Kashmir blanket under an old oak tree talking strategy, looking at the big picture — mergers, managerial theories, bogeys and birdies. You stand at the edge of their blanket, grinning sheepishly, your head slightly bowed to acknowledge their dominance. This gets you an invitation to share their iced tea and Fig Newtons. Now that you've got Osgood's ear you. . .

12

Make a bold move and suggest that you are just the person to head up the corporate diversification study — turn to page 20.

Or play it cool, decide to butter him up first, and invite him to your home for dinner — turn to page 22.

Top management initially balks at your idea for a company baseball league, but you win them over by convincing them that it will promote the health of their employees and also foster a spirit of teamwork. They also realize that it will provide another distraction, useful for keeping the union out.

In the opening game you manage one team and Snodgrass leads the other. The company has supplied the equipment and the beer and has made only one stipulation: the word "strike" is not to be used. The umpires will discreetly refer to such pitches as "not-balls."

Your side falls behind by one run. When one of your junior accountants draws a walk, you give her the steal sign. She makes it safely to second standing up. You're not entirely comfortable with the idea of an accountant who steals so easily, but you'll let it pass.

The executive vice-president for subsidiary operations comes to bat and not-balls out. Then you send yourself in as a pinch hitter and get a single. Snodgrass, your nemesis, has put himself in as the second baseman for the other side. With larceny (and a touch of murder) in your heart, you take off to steal second. Your spikes catch him on the seat of his pants as he turns to take the throw from the catcher. Even if Snodgrass someday becomes CEO, he will never sit in the CEO's chair.

Now you call for another pinch hitter. He hesitates, claiming that there's nothing in his job description about being second string. With the entire board of directors watching, you call the recalcitrant aside and apply every dirty little trick you ever learned about leadership psychology. Within two minutes he thinks it's in his interest to give you anything you want. He goes to bat, gets a hit, and wins the game.

It's hardly the playing fields of Eton, but maybe the activities on this sandlot can provide you with a metaphor for suc-

cess in your career. The problem is, what lesson should you draw from the game? Is it that individuals need to be sacrificed for the good of the team, or that teamwork depends on the creation of feelings of identification and belonging?

15

If it's going to be the company **uber alles**, and you decide to look good by hiring an efficiency expert to study your department and clear away dead wood, turn to page 39.

If instead you think it's more important to promote teamwork by re-creating the spirit of those glorious days of summer camp when it was all for one and one for all and the last one in the lake was a rotten egg, turn to page 26.

Finance and Accounting, with its low ceiling, reminds you of a crawl space. What better place to grovel? It simply means that you will have to stoop to conquer.

On your first day you meet the lady who collects for charities and sells raffle tickets. She seems to be perpetually in mourning. You say, "Hi, nice weather we're having," and she sighs: "It's a great life if you can bear it." They call her "Our Lady of the Sorrows." This week she's collecting for the Sisterhood of the Plague, Pestilence, and Poverty.

Your first assignment here is bizarre. You are asked to chair a committee that will determine if the company money maven will be called the "controller" or the "comptroller." For this you needed an MBA? Nevertheless, you want to get along, so you go along.

Frank Snodgrass — who, you are sure, also wants to be CEO — tries to dominate the committee meetings, pushing for "comptroller" because such a person would be "compellingly competent at computing." This birdbrain will bear watching.

The leaves on the decision tree you draw up are turning brown and beginning to fall by the time you push your colleagues to the conclusion you had in mind in the first place.

If you opt for "comptroller," turn to page 118.

If it's to be "controller," turn to page 6.

You get so absorbed in office politics that you can't even remember from one minute to the next what your company produces. Nor do you really care. To hell with productivity; it's who you know that counts.

The corporate low road has its disadvantages. The view isn't great and there are a lot of potholes. But there's no speed limit and you can get to the top quickly if you avoid head-on collisions. So you plan a route through rumor, manipulation, secrets, gossip, and alliances. You avoid direct confrontations by maneuvering other people into banging heads.

A day at your office begins to resemble a scene from **Othello** or **Richard III**: nonstop conniving. You, of course, officially stay above it all. Thank goodness for your assistant, Bill Sneed. He was a fencing champion at college; his specialty was the freehand back-stab. It's certainly not for his rapierlike wit that he's your deputy.

"My antennae are picking up something significant," Sneed portentously remarks one morning before you've had your second cup of coffee.

"It seems that Moynihan over in Advertising is hatching some kind of plot.

"Yeah," you shoot back. "But is it a scheme that could prove to be useful to us, or are they just going to lay an egg?"

"All I know for sure is that she and the distribution manager are spreading a rumor that a takeover attempt is imminent. They hope this will make the marketing operations manager either look for greener pastures or prematurely demand a Golden Parachute, thus demonstrating a lack of confidence in and loyalty to top management. That would get him out of their way."

Moynihan would also like to sit in the high-backed chair. That's clear enough. She's also on to your ambitions, and your point man is beginning to rub her the wrong way. Two days later she complains to you about him:

"Sneed seems to have a need to be snide."

You nod knowingly and innocently murmur, "Sneed, indeed."

"It's those asides."

"Asides?"

"Yeah," she confides, "the snide asides."

"Sneed's snide asides aside," you counter, "I hear that something is brewing around here besides coffee."

"Well, as a matter of fact, there's something you should know — something **big** is about to blow. It concerns an impending takeover attempt."

"Oh?" you remark, feigning great surprise.

18

Turn to page 31.

Osgood likes your suggestion for corporate diversification. "Variety is the spice of life, I always say," Osgood always says.

You gather a few trusted people from your division to help with your task — and one untrustworthy individual, Snodgrass, so that he'll be where you can keep an eye on him. Each person is to investigate a different area of potential corporate expansion and report back to you with his conclusions.

Bill Foster, chief of financial projections, revs up his computer and prepares a spreadsheet analysis of the pros and cons of purchasing a company in an allied field as opposed to branching out into an entirely new area. By posing a series of "what if . . ." questions, he'll demonstrate the effect of several different paths of corporate expansion on the cash flow, market position, and public image of the company. Seventy-two hours of computer time, seventeen reams of fanfold paper, and three worn and discarded accountants later, he declares that the figures point inexorably toward one conclusion: contraction.

"Numbers," he reminds you, "do not lie."

"And dead men," you reply, only half facetiously, "tell no tales."

Snodgrass, naturally, thinks he has a plan that will knock out IBM and EXXON. He reads to you from a newspaper clipping with the headline "Gun Fires Chicken at Planes." The chicken gun "is a converted twenty-foot cannon that shoots four-pound chickens into engines, windshields, and landing gear to determine how much damage such collisions can cause."

Snodgrass's plan calls for cornering the market on chicken guns by setting up a new, vertically integrated company division called SPLAT. The company, he reminds you, already has the facilities to produce the cannon. All that will be needed is the acquisition of a few chicken farms and some fried-chicken restaurants to recycle the spent ammunition.

Foster thinks it's a bold suggestion and commends Snodgrass for his pluck, but you cry fowl. You tactfully suggest to Snodgrass that he might want to invest in one of those correspondence courses that teach you how to be a person.

If you still think that corporate expansion will propel you to the top, turn to page 32.

If you think that diversification is beginning to sound like multifarious malarkey, turn to page 51.

You get the dinner commitment from Osgood, but setting a date is another matter. In fact, it takes several months of dealing with several layers of secretaries before you can circle a date on the calendar.

Finally, on an evening in early December, the doorbell rings, and out of the slush onto your white wall-to-wall carpet steps Mr. Osgood. Just as he tells you that his wife couldn't make it, your cat emerges from behind the umbrella stand, looks Osgood up and down, and throws up on his shoes.

Somehow you survive this entrance and get him to the table. Your self-effacing corporate wife is the model hostess, dressed in her tasteful skirt, correct blouse, and sensible shoes. Except for the twist of lemon she puts in Osgood's scotch and the off-vintage Château Gauche wine that tastes less as if it came from a cellar than from someone's sub-basement, you're proud of the dinner she serves. Besides, Osgood insists that he just loves blackbird pie.

Osgood is in such a mellow mood that he offers you a new position in which you will report directly to him.

If you look before you leap and say you'll think about it over the holidays and make a decision before the first of the year, turn to page 35.

If you jump at the opportunity, turn to page 37.

22

You are the liaison between your company and the ad agency that will promote Mock Teeth. Presentations are made by Young & Rubican and G. Falter Simpson, but you decide to go with Baitenhook, Creedmore (a swell bunch of guys), because they bought you the nicest lunch and made lots of jokes about "chewing on it for a while" and really "sinking their teeth" into the account.

Baitenhook has set up an ambitious market research operation. Peoria is their sample market, and they have sent a veritable army of vigorous retirees into town to ensure that every third geriatric fills out a questionnaire and every fifth submits to a field interview. (Your people have been cautioned not to use unnecessary force.)

The questionnaire is a dandy. It was carefully designed to plot the local denture demand curve and statistically determine the oral regression coefficient. You feel good about the sample questions you are shown:

1. When you throw caution to the winds, you eat:
- **a)** jelly apples
- **b)** rock candy
- **c)** watermelon rind

2. When you exercise, you:
- **a)** jog
- **b)** lift weights
- **c)** blow bubbles

3. When you get together with friends, you:
- **a)** Shoot the breeze
- **b)** trade stories
- **c)** chew the rag

4. Of these movies, the one you liked best was:
- **a)** Ghandi
- **b)** Tootsie
- **c)** Jaws

5. Of the following, you identify most with:
- **a)** Calvin Coolidge
- **b)** Marcel Marceau
- **c)** Fidel Castro

You love Baitenhook's print media ads for Mock Teeth. That great-grandmother with the toothy grin flexing her biceps and bragging, "Charged up, chipper, and still chewing," might go over big. But even better is the old codger leaning against the barn, whittling, and remarking out of the side of his mouth; "You don't have to worry anymore about eatin' apples. Hell, you can chew on cement."

25

If you sign off on the ads, turn to page 40.

If a little birdie in your head chirps "no, no," turn to page 42.

Still basking in the glow of your exploits on the baseball diamond, you recall those glorious years of your adolescence when you learned team spirit on the playing fields of Camp From-a-Hunger. Why not bring some of that **esprit de corps** into Finance and Accounting? Bringing about group identification will mark you as a man with leadership potential, a prime candidate for CEO.

The Friday after the softball game you let your people off early and throw a beer blast. You encourage them to come up with a wild and crazy motto for the department and a logo to put on arm patches and decal tattoos. They choose "In God we trust. All others pay cash." Their logo is an affirmation of their work ethic: a gold brick resting on a featherbed.

That weekend you write the group song, to the tune of "The Battle Hymn of the Republic":

> Our eyes have seen fake debits,
> Phony credits, furtive looks.
> We are great at double-dealing
> And we've kept two sets of books.
> We've padded our expenses
> And we've laundered fifty thou.
> Now the company till runs dry.
>
> Cheers for Finance and Accounting!
> Cheers for Finance and Accounting!
> Cheers for Finance and Accounting!
> Now the company till runs dry.

If you take this straight to the CEO to impress him, turn to page 100.

If you think this is too good to waste on this place, and decide that you would do better as a corporate morale consultant, turn to page 79.

26

Sales promos are iffy propositions — they can break as well as make a product. Plain table salt, for example, was set back several centuries by Lot's wife. She was supposed to be portraying a pillar of **strength**, but she missed her cue, got distracted, and turned away from the camera. The rest is history — who wants a product tied to Sodom and Gomorrah?

On the other hand, a well-done promotion is a thing of beauty forever. When the first white men climbed Mount Everest, only to find the perfectly preserved remains of a collard greens and chitlin dinner at the peak, the commercial success of frozen soul food was assured.

You should be so lucky. Everyone you speak to has a sure-fire idea about how to promote your product. Put a giant mock-up of Mock Teeth across George Washington's mouth on Mount Rushmore, urge some; string a chain of Mock Teeth across the mouth of the Mississippi, say others.

Finally you get a flash of insight. Aging people are sometimes referred to as "getting long in the tooth." That's insulting. What better way to promote Mock Teeth than to link them to an animal celebrated for being "long in the tooth"?

If you bet your money on an elephant's tusks, turn to page 43.

If you try to make your point with a saber-toothed tiger, turn to page 54.

You tell Moynihan that she's part of a class operation. "How do I get a piece of this action?" you ask.

"Prove yourself," she challenges. "Show your true colors."

If you were actually to do that, she would see a very bright shade of yellow. But you stifle your anxiety and rise to the occasion. You write "Up the Revolution" on the men's room wall and then start a rumor that the company is adding saltpeter to the split-pea soup in the employees' cafeteria. You also draw a moustache on the portrait of the company's founder that hangs just outside the executive sauna.

Moynihan is impressed; you are now a co-conspirator. As a matter of fact, you begin to enjoy the caper. It certainly is a quick way to reach the top. Why didn't **you** think of it?

As conspirators, your new comrades are rank amateurs. They don't even have a secret password. You take care of that. The word will be "proxy," to be countersigned with "moxy." Then, too, there should be some inconspicuous way of warning a fellow plotter of danger. You recall that grotesque mnemonic device they taught you in B-school for recalling the main aims of advertising: attention, interest, desire, and action. The first letters spell out AIDA. You pick your favorite aria from the opera of the same name and teach it to your new friends. As Zero Hour approaches, the company corridors begin to sound like backstage at the Met.

As for your slithery assistant, Bill Sneed, asking him to join any conspiracy is a mere formality. Does Sneed want to get involved in a plot? Does a worm like dirt?

Top management has already approached Sneed to do a little snooping for them. Having been apprised of this, you decide to use him as a counterspy, since he's a natural for the role of a mole. You order him to take Osgood's administrative assistant to lunch — buy her **two** Whoppers **and** fries — and let her know that there's mischief about the premises and

that he's willing to keep her informed. But he'll feed her false information with the all-beef patties — at least until you decide which is the right side to come down on.

Zero Hour is in two weeks. Plans are already being made to install a new CEO. To avoid a clash among themselves, the conspirators decide to offer the post to Lee Iacocca. You make a show of going along with this, but you really have other plans for that position. In the spirit of selflessness and service, you will be available for the job when the time comes.

If, finally, you are gung ho, and feel that you can coup with the best of them, turn to page 46.

But if on the other hand you're beginning to feel morally adrift, turn to page 45.

Moynihan wasn't kidding. There really is going to be a "take-over" — with a vengeance.

"We've decided to take executive action," she boasts. You're not sure what she's getting at, but with a little prodding she fills you in.

"Ben Arnold, the distribution manager, has recruited disaffected junior execs from Market Planning and Credit and has managed to assemble a hard core of cadres. Ben will pull his truck fleet off the road at Zero Hour and surround corporate headquarters. Corporate Security is in on this, too; they will seal off all entrances and exits. The lines from the PBX to the outside will be cut and, simultaneously, a message of greetings from the Paisley Liberation Front — that's us — will appear on every computer terminal in the building."

My God, you think, these bozos are actually planning a coup.

"We should have no trouble setting up a new regime," she goes on. "We've studied **The Zen Manual of Corporate Karate**: 'Grab them by their Xerox machines and their hearts and minds will follow.'"

"But what do you plan to do with top management?" you ask incredulously. "What happens to Charles Evans Osgood, the CEO?"

"They'll be taken care of," she remarks ominously. "The stationery supply room will be used as a detention center. Osgood will be issued a Golden Parachute without a ripcord and then pushed out a window."

You are all for character assassination, but this is a bit much.

If you decide to snitch, turn to page 34.

If you join the plot to see what you can learn, turn to page 28.

The diversification plan you finally accept is proposed by Helen Burton, a bookkeeper. Instead of just mouthing off, she's done her homework. Cable TV is where it's at, she reports. You commend her for her work, immediately have her transferred to the most distant branch office you can locate, and present her idea to Osgood as yours.

Osgood is delighted, thinks you're a fine fellow, and within a few months negotiates the purchase of a cable station, of which you are made the head. Administering Home Pox Office, "the station that grew from a tiny germ of an idea to a whole culture of culture," brings you some well-earned perks: occasional use of a limo, a corner office, and flatware rather than plastic utensils in the company cafeteria. From your window, on a clear day, you can see across into the CEO's office in the next wing.

HPO is hot stuff, mainly due to a prime-time soap opera called "General Ledger," designed to appeal to career climbers, and "The Bottom Line," a midnight nude financial panel discussion, aimed at the same lean and hungry group.

"General Ledger," a sprightly show in which anything can happen and usually does, is a successful combination of business antics with the traditional appeal of hospital melodrama. The story line involves the management of a for-profit hospital. Much fun is made of the unbalanced-sheet ward, where they keep the truly certified public accountants, and internal auditing, where executives are checked for ulcers. Needle-wielding nurses are forever joking with their patients about rapid turnover, and all patients are required to make an income statement as soon as they come in.

"The Bottom Line" is the station's biggest hit. Its nudity is nothing if not tasteful. In a brilliant format, two men and two women sit around and discuss price/earnings ratios, municipal bonds, and the like. The men wear wing-tipped shoes and the women, black pumps. The only four-letter words ever heard are "bull," "bear," and "bond."

As the years roll by, you have the satisfaction of knowing you're serving the public with quality programming, as well as enriching the company coffers. At first that touch of gray at your temples adds distinction, but then the gray begins to overwhelm the brown, leading to mid-fortyish thoughts of "what does it all mean?" and "where will it all end?" Is this all there is? Osgood has forced a change in company policy that makes him CEO for life. He is spiteful enough to live to a hundred. What do you do now?

33

If the appeal of naked midnights is fading for you and you think it's time for a shake-up, turn to page 59.

If you decide to make a daring move and have "The Bottom Line" panelists take off their shoes, turn to page 56.

Ah, treachery!

You sit in Osgood's office staring at the huge head of a male deer mounted on the Formica top of his solid oak desk, his colorful way of saying "The buck stops here." A push-button pneumatic jack under Osgood's chair enables the boss to look down on whoever is sitting across from him.

You have second thoughts as you stare up into two sets of vacant gray eyes — Osgood's and the deer's. Should you tell a cock-and-bull story to throw Osgood off the scent, thus aiding the managerial revolution, or should you go through with your planned betrayal? Are you, in the final analysis, pinko or Pinkerton?

You tell all. You haven't had so much self-righteous fun since as a hall monitor in junior high school you turned in two of your closest friends for smoking in the bathroom.

If you feel good about what you've done, relieved that you can at last come out of the closet and reveal yourself to be the fink you always knew you were, turn to page 49.

But if spilling the beans gives you **agità**, turn to page 50.

Taking the job would make you one of Osgood's boys; it would mean climbing aboard his ship. What if it turned out to be the **Titanic**? Too much hesitation, on the other hand, might also sink you. You feel like a pin-striped Prince Hamlet as Christmas — and decision day — closes in.

Meanwhile, Snodgrass is once again on the prowl. He's done a cost/benefit analysis of the annual office Christmas party and concluded that productivity would be best served by dropping the party and instead issuing all employees an apple and a festive slice of American cheese, with a request that in the spirit of giving they voluntarily put in a little overtime that evening. But Osgood, to whom birdbrain brings his brilliant scheme, offers a countersuggestion. Snodgrass can shut up and crawl back into his cubbyhole or be issued a special company franchise to sell apples on the nearest streetcorner.

The Christmas party does go on . . . and on. Herman Scriptenbaum, whose job is to operate the machine that stamps the treasurer's signature on all company checks, attempts to consummate his long-suppressed lust for accountant Emilia Philpott by launching some guided mistletoe over her head. Mistaking her nervous attempt to jerk her head away for approval, Scriptenbaum grabs for her across the punch bowl and they both end up in the drink.

Unfortunately, much of the drink is also ending up in you. Through your increasingly hazy perspective, you dimly perceive Snodgrass across the room next to the peanut butter and eggplant canapés, wildly gesticulating. Is he choking on his food? It seems so. Selflessly, you stumble to your rival's assistance. Grabbing him from behind, you vigorously administer the Heimlich Maneuver. Snodgrass, who is not choking at all, but rather is in the midst of telling a long and tasteless dirty joke, lets out a terrible scream as you inadvertently tear the cartilage in both his shoulders.

Snodgrass will live, but not well, For the next several weeks his arms will be held above his head by splints, thus forcing him to walk around in a pose of abject surrender. You, however, have little to gloat about. You no longer have to agonize about whether or not to accept Osgood's job offer. The decision has been made for you. A notice on your desk the day after Christmas informs you that you are being transferred to Sales. The company has recently acquired a firm that makes dehumidifiers, and you are being given the Arizona territory.

The End

Osgood did not get to be CEO by being Mr. Nice Guy. He's been using that "report direct to him" line for years to blunt potential challenges from young upstarts. All over the company, junior executives lose valuable work time while they write those reports. Having written your first, you are shocked to discover, when you deliver it, that there is nothing special about the in-box set up for your precious words. It's one of approximately a hundred similar ones covering one wall from floor to ceiling.

As a matter of fact, you're not even reporting directly to Osgood. His "office" is really a front, a kind of company mail drop. His real office is at some other, undisclosed place in the building.

You are a young cynic, disillusioned by your first encounter with corporate gamesmanship. You try to return to the wonderful world of payables and receivables as if nothing had happened, but all the zip has gone out of it.

Eventually you leave the business world entirely, intent on pursuing a forbidden adolescent fantasy. To have given voice to it as a youth would have automatically branded you a dork. For you, in your heart of hearts, lusted after something that others would only have accepted as a booby prize if they could not get into medical school. Now you will fulfill that secret desire. You will become a dentist.

The End

38

Seizing the initiative, you arrange for an efficiency survey of Finance and Accounting. Your subordinates fear for their jobs. You reassure them, pointing to the slogan on the cover of the efficiency company's brochure: "The company that wears its heart on its sleeve." Then why, they ask, does the drawing under the slogan show a bouncer type with his sleeves rolled up?

You'll deal with their qualms some other time. You've made the appointment, and two days later, Stephanie Chronos, the efficiency surveyor, arrives. Within twenty minutes she's completed the first half of her study and isolated a major productivity impediment in your office: scribe scrape. Most of your people spend most of their time writing — in ledgers, in appointment books, on bathroom walls, and the like. Unknowingly, they drag their elbows against the writing surface as they scribble, producing friction that results in the loss of several thousand man/woman work hours a year.

"Traditionally," Chronos explains, "this has called for the application of elbow grease. The early industrialists had access to privately produced elbow grease, but most of those sources have long since dried up." Some companies try to improvise, she says. "I've seen just about everything used as a substitute — Vaseline, K-Y Jelly, chicken fat, you name it. We prefer an exclusive homebrew — known only to us — that's batch-processed behind a luncheonette in Lubbock, Texas: office-grade Greasy Special #1. I'll order you a batch."

39

If you put all your faith in Chronos's efficiency study and assume that it's your ticket to the top, turn to page 65.

If you think that Chronos didn't go far enough and that the company needs to be overhauled by a return to the old Protestant work ethic, turn to page 60.

The campaign, which produces several million dollars in billing for Baitenhook, Creedmore, breaks just before Halloween, when oldsters are likely to have fond memories of dunking for apples.

The ads go over big. Americans begin to whistle the jingle after only a few weeks of TV exposure. They even go out to the kitchen for a snack in the middle of sitcoms so they won't miss any part of the commercial. The actors in the ads are besieged with offers to do soap operas. Schoolkids recite the lines by heart to each other.

There's just one problem. People are enamored of the ads, but they don't buy the product. The campaign is an artistic success and a commercial fiasco.

The company, by way of dehiring you, assigns you to a daily inspection of every broom closet in the building and requires that you report on your findings.

40

The End

Fortunately, you insisted that market research continue right up to the product-release date. On a hunch, you even hold Mock Teeth back for a few weeks. Sure enough, the last survey catches the beginning of a tidal change in opinion among older people. A decade after the natural look hit the rest of America, it finally reaches the elderly. Artificial teeth are on their way out; glamorous gums are in.

Health-food stores are desperate for a product to meet this new need. Thanks to you, your company is quick to retool, and within months you have "Goody Gum Drops" ready for market. This all-natural sucking candy, flavored with 100-proof rum and wheat germ for a "pleasantly nutty" taste, contains carotene, an organic coloring agent, which will do for gums what sun lamps do for skin. **Advertising Age** and **The Wall Street Journal** sing your praises. Your board of directors is singing a whole opera about you, and your making it to CEO is a foregone conclusion.

The End

Your promotion is carefully planned. Your market research analysts have come up with a detailed psychological profile of older people and have matched it against the appeal of various symbols. An elephant turns out to be an excellent match. Its skin is wrinkled, thus promoting age identification. The animal is known for its sharp memory, which serves as a counterbalance to the cruel stereotype of the senile senior citizen. And as if that weren't enough, many old people are Republicans.

Your plan is to have an elephant open a shopping center in Hannibal, Missouri, the heartland of America. National TV coverage will be assured by the elephant's rider, an eighty-seven-year-old great-grandmother with a black belt in karate. The elephant will follow the local high school marching band, which will employ several oversized Mock Teeth as castanets. Each kid in the band will wear a mask with the image of a smiling octogenarian, as will the kid who follows the elephant with a shovel.

Your company's management biggies have flown in with you the night before the big event, and in a midnight conference, one of the VPs cautions that "the best laid plans of mice and men . . ."

How prophetic. You've laid your plans; a local mouse has laid his. The next day the rodent emerges from a deli just as the parade passes. Mouse and elephant eyeball each other. It's no contest.

PACHYDERM PANICS: PLOWS PATH THROUGH PLAZA, the headlines

scream. A feature story describes how "Angry Mob Mocks Mock Teeth." Never mind, CEO, you're lucky you're not D-E-A-D.

The End

You are having second thoughts. Is this conspiracy really necessary? You recall your parents' precept: "Be nice." Why can't everybody be nice? Why can't we all be friends?

In your long dark night of the soul you return to your alma mater, the Whartown School of Finance at the University of Philadelphia, to consult with one of your profs, Solomon Hacker. His course, Conflict Resolution, has been a legend for several generations of students, who remember it fondly as "Head-Banging 101." You still recall the words carved above the classroom door: "Let's Split the Difference."

Hacker's unique method of bringing parties together to resolve disagreements — "kidney arbitration," he calls it — was first received with derision, but has since made its way into the textbooks. The method is elegant in its simplicity: Lock them in without access to a bathroom until they reach an agreement.

Prof. Hacker is willing to get on your case himself, but he points out that his past relationship to you might make some people view him as less than objective. If you're worried about that, he can recommend a good conciliation service.

If you think Hacker can hack it, turn to page 53.

If you choose the service, turn to page 58.

45

You're determined to perfect your ability to read as well as speak body language. In order to achieve a satisfactory level of proficiency, you concentrate on picking up at least one sign from everyone you speak to during the day.

At first you marvel at your ability to spot hidden messages all around you. Before long you are speed-reading your way around the office. The only problem is that you can't turn it off; you can't stop at one level of meaning for each person. You are picking up subtexts, physical footnotes, subtle allusions that come from, say, observing the bend of an elbow, even when the main statement is set forth with folded arms. And you're unable to confine it to your colleagues. The elevator, coffee shop, supermarket, and tennis court are hotbeds of hostility, doubt, envy, ambivalence. You're picking up messages left and right, hand over foot.

Within weeks you're in big trouble. You can't concentrate; you're caught up in a cacophony of body-language babble. You're conscious of the hidden utterances of so many selves that the weight of the world is falling on your increasingly rounded shoulders.

In desperation you try to talk it out with a close friend, but when he nervously puts his hand on the back of his head, it's the last straw. You're led away screaming.

The End

There's a coup in the air. Top management has noticed that the absentee rate for Fridays and Mondays has decreased suddenly and that the company suggestion box has been virtually empty — no obscene notes or wacko ideas for a change, just a few losing pari-mutuel tickets. But although the company knows something is going on, they don't know just what.

Should something happen, CEO Charles Evans Osgood and his lieutenants are not without the means to defend themselves. A few years ago, in response to several incidents of industrial espionage, part of the company's security police was reorganized into a crack special-forces unit. They look truly fearsome in their Calvin Klein fatigues, crew cuts, and puce berets.

To intensify the rapidly growing paranoia in the executive suite, you send the CEO an anonymous cryptic message: "BEWARE THE IDES OF MARCH. COVER YOUR ASSETS." By God you're getting to enjoy this; you'll be sorry when it's over. You haven't had so much fun since you passed the final in Business Ethics by using a crib sheet you had concealed under your loose fingernail.

Sneed is also getting into it, perhaps too much. He spends half his time in front of a mirror practicing furtive looks and insists on being called Dmitri. You will have to have him watched. But what do you call a spy who spies on a counterspy? That's it! You'll have him tailed by an over-the-counter spy.

Having taken care of that, you sit back and await Zero Hour, knowing that before it's all over you and your colleagues will have determined Time's cover story for that week. If you win, you'll be described as "innovative corporate statesmen"; if you lose, you'll be "conniving Bolsheviks."

You win! The old fogies give in without a fight. The conspirators, in a gesture of goodwill, snap a pair of golden handcuffs on Osgood and let it go at that. He and the rest of the old guard are flown into exile in northern Idaho, where they are to be confined indefinitely on an underground golf course.

In a surprise move, Lee Iacocca declines the position of CEO. Having rescued an all but moribund Chrysler, he has now been engaged to raise the **Titanic** and will have no time for trivial pursuits.

That should make it easy for you. In the executive conference room, around a table laden with Cutty Sark, Fritos, and guacamole dip, you humbly suggest that you are open to a draft. Unfortunately, no one listens. Instead, they heed Sneed, who is spinning out a self-serving theory concerning the need to choose a CEO who is universally mistrusted, thus forcing all concerned to keep on their toes in order to prevent the establishment of a tyrannical regime.

You're incredulous when they actually go for this drivel. You have lost an assistant as well as an opportunity to be CEO, beaten out by a snake in the grass.

The End

Osgood listens impassively as you dig the dirt. Is he thinking? Sleeping? Dead? But when you've finished, he immediately buzzes his secretary: "Ms. Grundy, I'm going to give you the names of several nogoodniks. Call the Human Resources Fringe Benefits Department and have them cancel these miscreants' stock options and discount squash-court time. Then show them the door."

From now on there is no doubt about the identity of Osgood's heir apparent. You are the fair-haired boy.

Of course, there is some fallout from the whole sordid incident; the conspirators, after all, did have many friends in your division. You find yourself docked from the office betting pool and for several weeks there is always something weird on your desk when you arrive in the morning. One day it's a dead canary, another it's thirty pieces of silver.

Nevertheless, your career in Marketing proceeds apace. You scatter the bodies left and right over the years as you maneuver your way up the career ladder to Marketing VP. When Osgood retires, you fulfill your ambition and are chosen CEO, only to discover an ugly little secret. The conspirators knew what they were doing. Osgood was a crook who was systematically embezzling millions from the company, which is now on the verge of bankruptcy. You have become the captain of a sinking ship.

The End

49

The joy of snitching is short-lived. The plot was a ruse, a Corp-scam in which Osgood and the board of directors, through an elaborate entrapment scheme, were trying to ferret out disloyal elements in the company. Everyone else saw through it. Only you got suckered.

Boy, don't you look stupid. You no longer need worry about whether or not you will become CEO. After this, you're lucky if they let you clean the executive washroom.

The End

Maybe variety is the spice of life, but you wish life would go easier on the hot peppers. This diversification business is beginning to upset your stomach.

Getting to the top by climbing up the side of the corporate pyramid may not be worth the toll it's taking on you. Perhaps you could achieve the same end by boring up from within. That's it! You'll pull off an inside job. You'll curry favor, accumulate political IOUs, gather goodwill, develop a loyal following, and finally be swept into the CEO's chair by a rising tide of love and affection from your peers.

Ruthlessly you begin to go about the business of acquiring that love and affection. You read Abraham Maslow on everyone's hierarchy of needs, study monographs on job enrichment in **The Harvard Business Review**, and discover how you can be perceived to be kind, generous, thoughtful, helping, and caring, all the while being nothing more than subtly manipulative.

All this calls for some heavy role-playing. Through a little trial and error, you find just the right role: the office priest-psychiatrist. You encourage everyone to come to you with his problems, both business and personal. You're a fiendishly good listener, and discover that you have a knack for making people think they feel better about themselves after talking to you. Even Snodgrass.

"You know, I think I have never forgiven myself for cheating my pal Billy in the lemonade stand we set up when we were ten years old," birdbrain says to you one day.

"And how do you **feel** about it now?" you prod cleverly.

"Anguished, guilty, filled with remorse," he only too anxiously acknowledges. "But I also feel better having told you and gotten it off my chest." Your contempt for him is now absolute.

This and similar exchanges make you feel very powerful.

You accumulate dirt on many of your rivals. You encourage them to become dependent on you until you have them just where you want them.

Within a few years your reputation has spread throughout the company. Every morning there is a line of unfortunates outside your office waiting for counseling. Top management has noticed these strange goings-on, but does nothing because you have unwittingly pacified many of the company malcontents.

If you think this is getting you closer to CEO and you intend to stay put and keep on listening, turn to page 57.

If you're beginning to think that CEO is small cheese when someone with your talent could be making big bucks outside in the therapy business, turn to page 113.

No sweat. Hacker is acceptable to everyone and the company hires him immediately. He begins his mediation with a Kissinger ploy. With the disputants in separate rooms at either end of a long corridor, he practices shuttlecock diplomacy, passing messages back and forth. You can get dizzy watching him make like a birdie.

Finally Hacker has both conspirators and old guard in the same room. He locks the door, opening it only for the enormous quantities of beer he keeps ordering from the local deli, knowing that soon there will be several sets of kidneys primed to go off like Old Faithful. Within two hours, amid increasingly nervous glances, he gets both sides to agree to binding arbitration. He proposes tentatively that the company be split up in the manner of AT&T, the conspirators to get Research and Development, the old guard to control Production and Distribution. Osgood, who at this point is all but incontinent, quickly gets his colleagues to agree. But Moynihan, speaking for her side, says, "There are those who love this old company, and they don't want to see it split in two."

That's all Solomon Hacker needs to hear. "Control of the entire company is awarded to the conspirators," he says almost immediately. "It's obviously their baby."

You could swear you've heard of such a decision before, but you can't place it. No matter. Moynihan is chosen CEO by acclamation. The king is dead; long live the queen.

And you? You've gotten the royal screw.

The End

Wrong move. This tiger boosts your product like poison cap-sules promoted Tylenol.

Your plan had been to stage a jelly-apple-eating contest between the oldest tiger in the Dingaling Brothers' Circus and an old man fitted with Mock Teeth. The tiger is long in the tooth but short on patience. It takes one look at the oldster, pulls him into his cage, and eliminates the competition with one gulp.

As if this weren't disaster enough, the sideshow geek, whose idea of a good time is to swallow rusty nails and live lizards, swallows a pair of Mock Teeth and almost chokes to death.

You're the subject of several lawsuits, and criminal charges may be brought against you. You and the tiger both may soon be wearing stripes. Is there a CEO in prison?

The End

Stock market tips delivered bare-assed — and barefoot — it tickles America's fancy. The program's ratings climb. "Bottom Line" clubs form in all major cities. Merchandise tie-ins generate healthy profits. Fig leaves in the form of dollar signs do very well, as does **Over the Counter and Through the Woods**, a guide to nude upscale picnic areas.

You have long since given up all hope of succeeding Osgood and have just about settled for remaining on this plateau in life when suddenly it happens. Hugh Heifer's bunny empire, based on the men's magazine, **Say, Boy!**, is rumored to be tottering on the brink. Its board of directors, in a last-ditch effort to keep it from centerfolding, forcefully remove Heifer, place him under hutch arrest, and offer you his furry crown. When you least expect it, you at last become CEO.

The End

You become a phenomenon. **People** magazine does a three-page article on you called "Playing It by Ear: A Manager Who **Listens**." Aspiring industrial psychologists keep your home phone ringing off the hook with requests for interviews for their doctoral dissertations. Management textbooks take note, and before the age of forty you become a "case study." What you are doing is even given a name: The Empathy Ploy. It spawns a cottage industry of expensive books with big print that tell managers how to combine the best of Freud, Saint Paul, and Machiavelli — "three-facing," they call it.

But there are limits to your cynicism. All those sad personal stories are beginning to get to you. You're getting depressed, feeling burned out. And no one has given you the impression that Osgood's high-backed chair might yet be yours. Then one day you hear distant drums: A headhunter is calling.

57

If you heed the call, turn to page 62.

If you stay put, turn to page 119.

The Amiable Benevolent Conciliation Service is in a storefront in an old part of town. The director, a Mr. Michael Corleone, a serious-looking man in a dark suit, shakes your hand, holds up two fingers in the peace sign, and says, "Come, let us reason together." After introducing you to two of his associates, Mr. Tony Ducks and Mr. Sal the Barber, Mr. Corleone explains that his group specializes in final-offer arbitration, in which each side is encouraged to make an offer the other can't refuse. Should that fail, the service reserves the right to apply binding arbitration. "And if that doesn't work," Mr. Corleone adds affably, "we go to the mattresses." You assume that means the parties get some time to sleep on it.

The service also guarantees compliance by parties to an agreement as long as it's in effect. "Toward that end," Mr. Corleone explains, "we use noogs."

"Noogs? What's a noog?"

"Oh, just a contract enforcer," he replies. "A kind of informal referee whose decision shall be final, you might say."

Corleone seems reasonable, so you bring him in. What happens next occurs so quickly that it leaves you dizzy. In one long and bloody night, all the disputants are outplaced with extreme prejudice and Corleone appoints himself CEO. He's certainly more efficient than his predecessor, but at least you didn't have to kiss Charles Evans Osgood's ring and call him "Godfather."

The End

One day it finally hits you. You're a grown man, at the height of your powers, producing a TV program in which four naked people sit around talking about stocks and bonds. This is not what your mother raised you to do. In a swift move that sets the industry abuzz, you cancel the program with less than a week's notice and replace it for the rest of the season with a six-part documentary on snail farming.

All hell breaks loose. The creaky, moldy gentlemen on the board of directors of your company, popularly known as "the dirty old men," were very fond of "The Bottom Line." They have just returned from an outing to a porno movie house and have barely had time to put away their raincoats and settle down for their meeting when they hear the news. Their vengeance is swift. You will never, they assure you, become Chief Executive Officer of this company. In fact, just to make sure you get the point, they buy the porno movie theater and make you Chief Usher.

The End

It's ironic that Stephanie Chronos is recommending elbow grease. That's something from the old way of doing business, when companies were run by crusty old SOBs instead of wise-guy MBAs. Temperamentally, you are more in tune with the olden days.

As far as you're concerned, Chronos hasn't turned the clock back far enough. Elbow grease is just the beginning. What this company really needs is to start burning the midnight oil. Sure enough, you manage to locate a small firm in Boston that still makes the stuff from whale blubber, and you order a year's supply.

Not only do you encourage the pasty-faced bookkeepers in your division to continue using their goose quills, you issue ultimatums to everyone else: Fountain pens are to replace ballpoints. And those underutilized computers are to be removed from the premises. You have no use for any banks — data banks included — that don't take deposits or give loans.

For a long time you've been tired of holding the phone in one hand and a dictionary of abbreviations and acronyms in the other. Anyone using an acronym for anything from now on will be fined and publicly reprimanded.

You get so worked up in your enthusiasm to restore the gloomy good old days that when you learn the board of directors are holding their monthly meeting in the conference room right down the hall, you go storming over, throw open the door, barge in, pound on the table, and bellow that you're angry as hell and you're not going to take it anymore. "What ever happened to spunk and gumption?" You scream. "That's **spunk and gumption**, not SAG."

For a moment there is silence, and then the room rings with huzzahs. In truth, you have never heard so many huzzahs in one room. Osgood is issued his walking papers on the spot and you are elected CEO by acclaim.

The End

The headhunter, a Mr. Caput, is very friendly on the phone. He says he represents an overseas client who is very much in need of a manager-headshrinker. You agree to meet him at a Polynesian restaurant for lunch.

"Tell me about the company," you say to him as you pick through your poi.

"Well," he replies, "it produces jewelry, ornaments, and theatrical artifacts — masks, beads, costumes, and the like. And," he adds with a half-smile, "miniatures." Beyond that, he will not elaborate.

Caput seems to have read all the books on group behavior and organization. He speaks knowingly of his client's belief in traditionalism. "This company, you might say, is structured like an extended family; the CEO is known informally as 'Chief.' The firm's credo is 'hard work and sacrifice,' and the kind of person they usually are looking for must have a good head on his shoulders."

There's a certain vagueness in his response, but you press on. "And the competition?"

There is **no** competition," he replies, his face momentarily darkening.

"But what if it arises?"

He reflects for a moment, leans back, smiles slightly, and remarks ever so offhandedly, "Why then, they would just be eaten up."

You make it clear that your goal is to get ahead. You would not be satisfied remaining a mere spear carrier.

"Rest assured you will be at the center of things," Caput says. "Now, will you come?"

What the hell? "Yes."

"That's capital," he chortles. "Splendid."

The truth of the matter does not become clear until you're on the plane with him, heading out over the Pacific, and he slips a bone through his nose. In a few hours you will be either a living god or in hot water up to your neck.

The End

You just bought a ticket to nowhere. You have assumed too much without seeing the second half of Chronos's report.

The next morning, as you emerge from the elevator, you hear a swelling chorus of "For He's a Jolly Good Fellow." Snodgrass is singing the loudest. All your people have gathered in the aisle and pat you on the back as you make your way to your office. Snodgrass is standing in the doorway, all but drooling with pleasure as he hands you a gold watch.

What the hell is going on here? Someone points to a note on your desk from Ms. Chronos: "Sorry I had to miss your surprise retirement party, but one must make hay while the sun shines. I wrote my efficiency report last night, and I'm afraid that **you** turned out to be the odd man out. Nobody at the company seemed able to explain just what you **did**. I'm sure you'll understand."

No, you don't understand, but it no longer matters. You have been outplaced.

The End

You just tripped over the bottom line. In your first big decision, you bet on a turkey.

To ward off incipient depression, you take the advice you picked up from the best-selling book on Japanese management, **Theory ZZZZ**, and you sleep on it. You dream of a paper you wrote in B-school on "missionary" sales, in which a company sends salespeople to retailers to give pep talks about their products.

When you awake, suddenly it all falls into place. You compose a memo suggesting that your company's sales division be reorganized along the lines of a religious institution — the adoption of a "missionary posture," translated into corporatese. The company's huckster honchos go for it; they order Sales to give you their full cooperation. Only the saleswomen resist, claiming that the adoption of such a posture will relegate them permanently to the bottom.

67

If you accept an offer to supervise the reorganization of the sales division, turn to page 73.

If, on second thought, you decide that any real business decision you might make is not as important as the physical image you project at the company, turn to page 68.

There's a theory that it's neither who you are nor whom you know that counts, but rather how you look. The best method of clawing your way to the top may be to keep your nails manicured and concentrate on dressing down the opposition. Clothes make the man, they say.

Louie's, a branch of the famous Palermo haberdashery, is a real find. Louie himself came over three years ago to run it. His English is still shaky, but he's already demonstrated a vast knowledge of business — his and others'.

"What's new?" you whisper out of the side of your mouth, eager to pick up an exclusive.

"Divest," he replies.

"No kidding," you remark, mentally scanning the list of your company's subsidiaries for dead wood. "I wouldn't want our rivals to know our strategy. Maybe we could fake another move to cover up our true intentions."

"Yeah," says Louie, "you cover uppa divest witha disuit."

"Brilliant. I should have thought of it myself. We'll distract them by bringing suit. Patent infringement — that's a good one these days."

Louie just stands there staring at you, uncomprehending.

If you continue to feel that Louie's sartorial skill will have you dressed for the kill, turn to page 112.

But if on the other hand you're beginning to think your strong suit might be an office that reflects power and status, turn to page 70.

68

By now you've put in your time in Sales and paid some dues. With increased status and responsibility has come the right to occupy one of the five corner offices on your floor. You've already made an appointment to consult with the corporate interior decorator, Oscar de la Retcha, a corporate game player who needs to be watched and dealt with forcefully. He did you dirty when you were the new guy on the block. You ended up with an old school desk, complete with inkwell, located in a partitioned cubbyhole — partitions formerly used to section off the stalls in the old washroom.

Oscar, you discover, has since come up in the world. He's acquired a degree in Human/Environmental Relations — isn't that about how to talk to plants? — and he now blathers a good deal about "ergonomics."

You wave away Oscar's color chart, determined to lay down the law from the start. You've read **Let Your Office Work for You** and you know just what job this room is going to have.

"Paint it black," you order imperiously, knowing that will give you an image of mystery. "My desk is to be precisely in the middle of the room, far enough away from anything else so that visitors will feel insecure when they deal with me."

You order a collection of dead plants for the window to show that you have no time for trivia. You also demand fast-track lighting with optional strobe effects to disorient colleagues and customers.

You insist on having your own personal copier. "Sure," replies Oscar. "We can fit a Xerox in next to the imitation Naugahyde couch."

"No, you don't understand." You explain to him how you loved those Xerox TV commercials featuring Brother Timothy, the mild-mannered medieval monk who spends all of his time copying. In the ad he is rescued from yet another hand job by a Xerox. But you already have a Xerox, just like everyone else around here. What you want is your own personal monk. "They won't be putting **my** memos in the circular file — not when they arrive on parchment."

There remain only the final touches: a Chippendale computer table, a designer paper shredder, and a plaster cast of your feet to put up on the desk so that you can feign indifference even when you're out.

If, having toughened up your office, you're ready to toughen up your act, turn to page 74.

But if you think you may have traveled too far from your inner self, lost your sensitivity and need to get back in touch with your feelings, turn to page 77.

Since 1930, Americans have bought more than 25 billion Hostess Twinkies. They also bought Richard Nixon. There are virtually no limits to what a sales organization imbued with faith, spirit, and dedication can do.

You revamp the structure of your company's sales division, replacing regions, districts, and territories with dioceses and parishes. When your salespeople balk at taking vows of chastity and poverty, you remain adamant, although you relent on clerical collars and habits. You show them how to recast their pitches as sermons and meet customer resistance with the rejoinder that it is better for them to order your product than to burn in hell.

Personally, of course, you maintain a secular outlook. In the long run, it's not the miter but the crown you want to wear.

Over the next few years you pay your dues as an account executive and learn that in your line of work, the shortest distance between breakfeast and dinner is an all-day lunch. You learn it, but you don't always like it. It's hard to break down someone's sales resistance over pâté when they make perfectly plausible points as to why they shouldn't go for your slick pitch.

73

If you refuse to give in to your ambivalence and resolve to martini your way to the top, turn to page 81.

But if having to deal with the reality of your company's products leaves you completely frustrated and dries up your creative juices, turn to page 84.

You've secured your home port and are ready to set sail as a corporate corsair. But before you hoist the Jolly Roger, you must get your act together. You need something that will project a more powerful "you." What was it someone once said . . . ?

Your teachers in B-school were quote-crazy. If it wasn't some pithy apothegm from Peter Drucker, it was probably a pointed phrase from **The Peter Principle** or an equally distinctive dictum from some other Peter. Personally, you think all that quoting was a cover-up for the fact that your teachers themselves had nothing to say. Those who can, do; those who can't, quote.

There was, however, one quotation that stuck in your mind like a hungry bug on flypaper. You got it from a veteran of the corporate wars who claimed to have stared into the moral abyss of big business until it began to stare back at him. It was from Machiavelli: "If we must choose between them, it is far safer to be feared than loved."

The essential truth of this is brought home to you by an encounter with the people who exert enormous, but hidden, corporate power: the company cleaning women. Never mind the names in the annual report; the hand that holds the broom has its finger on the corporate pulse. Who else knows more about the dirt that's been swept under the rug?

Initially, you make the mistake of affecting an air of friendly condescension toward them, barely acknowledging their presence. A little ammonia under your desk at four-thirty clears that attitude out of your head and makes you sit up and take notice. Slowly, they begin to break down your morale by ordering you around the room; they always want to clean where you're standing. When you get a phone call, they distract you with their incessant gab, then humiliate you by spraying the phone with disinfectant as soon as you've finished your call. Finally they break your spirit by reading aloud from the papers on your desk, commenting sarcastically on your managerial style, referring to you as "him," as if you weren't there.

You are not slow on the uptake. They have taught you an important lesson — they do not for a moment accept your authority, they don't give a damn, they will not play your game. They leave you thinking that they are capable of doing anything.

You incorporate the cleaning-woman syndrome into your corporate style and push it to its ultimate limits. People must be kept off balance. Let them suspect that behind that businesslike demeanor there might, just might, be an ax murderer.

On your next vacation you indulge in a little plastic surgery that squares your jaw and narrows your eyes for a slightly cruel look. You take an assertiveness training course, and by the last week you even have the instructor frightened. You still have **The Wall Street Journal** and **Barron's** delivered to your desk, but you also get **Soldier of Fortune** and **The American Funeral Industry Diurnal Journal**. Just in case people don't get the point, the executive toy you keep on the desk is a loaded Magnum.

You have made your point. From now on, everyone gives you a wide berth. You are, after all, a wild and crazy guy.

76

76

If you think you have your act perfected and are ready to go one on one with one of your rivals for CEO, turn to page 80.

But if you think you need to be more objective and efficient and would rather use impersonal relations to process your enemies in a batch, turn to page 89.

You're not the only one at your company out of touch with your feelings. There are receptionists who've smiled so hard for so long that they require surgery to stop, and vice-presidents who've become so officious at the office that they're unable to switch gears and be familiar once they're home with their families.

Recognizing its responsibilities in this area, the company has hired an outside firm to help all of you find "the real me," for a fee. Group members learn how to be up-front and fill their lives with sincerity, authenticity, meaningfulness, and more money.

The group you join is led by Larry (leaders are known only by their friendly first names), who has achieved a third-degree Gucci belt in Zazenahchu, an ancient Oriental self-defense and weight-reduction technique. He is a former Jesuit and Hollywood producer who suddenly got in touch with **his** feelings one day while driving on the Santa Ana Freeway.

The encounter sessions are held in the quiet intimacy of a Hyatt Regency atrium. When you arrive for the first session, the others are already seated around Larry in a semicircle. You walk over to him, extend your hand, and say "Hi."

"I feel that you are being hostile," Larry responds in a monotone, looking you straight in the eye.

What **you** are feeling is that he is either a fool or a lunatic. You can feel yourself becoming less sensitive by the minute.

"I don't seem to be able to relate well to my work environment and my colleagues," Henrietta Haagendazs, an icy sales trainee, just then intones compulsively. She feels that she has a communications problem. "I read **I'm O.K., You're O.K.**, but it's still not okay. I apparently misread **Winning Through Intimidation**. I was under the impression that it advocated a reverse domination theory. I thought I was supposed to let myself get so intimidated that the person intimidating me would be overcome with guilt and be willing to do anything to earn my forgiveness — even surrender unconditionally. I also tried **How to Be Your Own Best Friend**, but I wasn't my type."

"Have you read **When Good Things Happen to Bad People**?" you ask, in an effort to be helpful.

"I feel that is subtly hostile," Larry once again chirps. "You need to work on being more up-front."

"Yes, it's hostile. And I **will** try to be more up-front," you declare forthrightly, now thoroughly in touch with your feelings. You get up, punch him in the nose, and leave.

If poking Larry's proboscis offers you no satisfaction, but rather leaves you feeling as if you are trying to punch your way out of a paper bag, turn to page 93.

On the other hand, if you think that getting physical is the only language they may really understand around here, turn to page 95.

You hire a staff of industrial psychologists to tell you how to manipulate workers' solidarity instincts; artists to design corporate flags, jackets, and T-shirts; wordsmiths to pen corporate jingles and fight songs; and an Indian contortionist to develop weird and complicated secret corporate handshakes. You devise a standard corporate color-war format and, in a real coup, hire away the Dallas Cowboy cheerleaders, who will be available for brief morale-building appearances and, you hope, will also get some of the bookings at fairs and parades that have been going to the Budweiser Clydesdales.

You started your business on a song and have managed to survive a lot of silly jokes about how you capitalized it with a few notes. But those who scoffed are now whistling a different tune; you are the CEO of a very successful company.

The End

Livingston Schermerhorn Joralemon III, Rhodes scholar and Harvard MBA, came to your company with a ticket good for nonstop success. The preppy par excellence, Joralemon was born with horn-rimmed eyebrows; his umbilical cord was an old school tie. His first words were "mother" and "father"; his next were "gin" and "tonic."

Joralemon is a comer, an odds-on favorite in the race for CEO. You hate him with a passion. Now that you are at your intimidating best, you're ready to do him in.

You've chosen the territory ploy. You begin by storing some cartons of **your** papers in **his** office space. Then you appropriate some of his file drawers. Next you move your work ahead of his at the secretarial pool. You do all of this in a matter-of-fact manner. That's the point: Make him feel it would be strange to so much as question your clearly aberrant behavior. That's the name of the intimidation game.

But you're unable to squelch him permanently, so you question his manhood and challenge him to see who can best hold his liquor at the Inn Box. After eight gin and tonics, he's still cool as a cucumber sandwich, but your loosened tongue has given away your game plan.

Just before you pass out, Joralemon reveals that he got his job through his uncle, Charles Evans Osgood, the current CEO.

You could swear that's a pink slip you see floating among the pink elephants. It looks so real. Better believe it.

The End

Sam Morgan, purchasing agent for Consolidated Con-glomeration, is making a whirlwind visit to the city — an opportunity for you to put some points on the corporate scoreboard. You've reconnoitered that snooty French res-taurant, Le Très Cher, and made the acquaintance of the maître d'. You're set to shine; this is going to be **un** business lunch **magnifique**.

Disaster! First the checkroom attendant rejects your imita-tion Burberry with disdain. Sam politely looks away. Then another **petite catastrophe**. The maître d' has the day off; his replacement doesn't know you from Yves Montand. He seats you at a table halfway between the men's room and the kitchen door, directly under the air conditioner. You're mak-ing quite an impression.

Having assured Sam that the filet of sole is the best in town, you call over the wine steward, who recommends a fine Chardonnay to go with the fish. You'll have no such thing. You give Sam a quick kvetch about nose, bouquet, and tannin, and then order a bottle of something unpronounce-able. It's also the most expensive vino on the list. The steward smirks, then disappears. Sam does not look pleased when a bottle of red Burgundy is later uncorked next to the fish.

C'est de mal en pis! That big order from Sam Morgan is fading as fast as Claude Rains in **The Invisible Man**. You'll have to recoup on the dessert. You wave away the pastry cart and tell the garçon that you'd like something prepared to order. You've got Sam's attention now. Also that of the waiter, who's watched this debacle as it's developed and can't wait to see what you come up with next. Slyly referring to your pocket phrase book, you shoot the works. "It's certainly interesting," Sam remarks kindly five minutes later, as the waiter sets down the brussels sprouts flambé.

If you decide to 'fess up to your pretentiousness and invite Sam to shmooze about business over some honest java and apple pie at the coffee shop in your office building, turn to page 98.

If you think that you can still come off the sophisticate by showing Sam some risqué nightlife, turn to page 88.

The problem with selling a product is that it's too tangible. No matter what you say about it, it's finally there to be judged. That limits your creativity.

Public relations, on the other hand, means never having to say you're sorry. It deals with an image, and there's little the image can be measured against. In this field you can say anything you damn well please and get away with it as long as you say it often enough.

Sales is pushing snake oil; PR is getting people to trust snakes.

You transfer to Public Relations just as the company's image-building is undergoing an overhaul. From now on, lies are to be replaced with myths, lowdown untruths with creative fictions. It's going to be an operation you'll be proud to be associated with.

84

If you want to head the committee to seek out and develop a new corporate image for the "benefit" of the general public, turn to page 86.

But if you think it's the company's employees who need to have the cashmere pulled over their eyes, turn to page 92.

You hope to do for your company what Herbert Schmertz did for Mobil. If Mobil Oil can get away with those cutsey-pie public-advocacy ads, the folksy ones that deliver the home-spun "musings of an oil person" on the op-ed pages of major newspapers, then anything is possible.

You work with an agency to come up with an effective slogan. There certainly are some good examples to serve as precedents. Even a multinational giant that includes weapons technology among its products can be made to appear familiar, warm, and cuddly — witness "a company called TRW." (The Soviet Union was so impressed with that one that they hired an American PR firm to make **them** look good, too. The campaign to dispel the half-truths and innuendos about "an agency called KGB" is set to break later this year.)

A market-research project tests hundreds of phrases. Finally, it comes down to "The company with its feet on the ground and its heart in its mouth." This suggests uprightness, solidity, humility, romance, and oral satisfaction.

A new image requires a fresh spokesperson, a public figure whose appeal will rub off on your company — someone like Bob "Texaco" Hope. But Hope is spoken for, and although Ronald Reagan's work at GE is admired by everyone, he's currently on another assignment. Johnny Carson is rejected because he will undoubtedly want to have a guest spokesperson stand in for him nine weeks a year.

The old company business card will have to go. The new card should evoke roots and a tradition, and there's nothing like a little Latin phrase to do just that. **Caveat emptor** is one you've heard around; you'll look up the meaning later. For a logo you want something identifiable, a symbol of both solidity and flexibility. The Leaning Tower of Pisa is perfect for the job.

But you hit a snag when you try to come up with a way to con the masses into thinking that your company is public-spirited. How do you do that for a firm like yours?

If you decide to buy public approval, and think that corporate philanthropy is the way to go, turn to page 108.

However, if you're more inclined to have your company perform good deeds directly, and you think that it's youth that must be served, turn to page 101.

At the Wine-by-the-Pint Cocktail Lounge, the bald business-man is king. You'll never forget that sale you closed when the buyer who thought he'd seen everything got to tie up one of the exotic dancers with municipal bonds.

You're leering, winking, and all but breaking Sam's ribs with the thrust of your elbow in an effort to apprise him of just how the tired businessman gets reinvigorated here. But it's not penetrating. This is a man who's probably never seen tassels except on the tops of executive loafers.

Sam still thinks that a bordello is a pizza that comes with the works. Okay, you'll humor him. You tip FiFi LaFemme to come over and give hime some meatballs, anchovies, **and** extra cheese. By the time you've rolled some oregano cigar-ettes and lit up, Sam's beginning to catch on.

Unfortunately, this party is about to get pooped. You left your American Express Gold Card at the French restaurant. When you try to pay cash, you are bluntly informed that that is not acceptable.

Sam has to wash dishes. You've lost the sale and will prob-ably lose your job. And you didn't even get a slice of that pizza.

The End

The computer is here! The computer is here! It arrived early this morning, and already three file clerks have been excessed.

When you were growing up, "feedback" was a sudden and dramatic reaction to the food in your high school cafeteria, "printout" was the way you were told to write your name at the top of an exam paper, and an "intelligent" copier was a person who knew whose paper to look at once the test began. No more. Computers are everywhere, and with them have come enough new buzz words to keep a whole hive of bees happy.

At this point you don't know a microchip from a chocolate chip, but you have a nose for the main chance, and your schnoz tells you that computers are where it's at. You're determined to become computer literate. You buy several paperbacks on the subject — way overpriced to ensure that only the better sort of people become computer literate — and over a period of two years take several advanced courses on the subject, absorbing the complicated data in small bytes.

You even buy a home computer. You break down and cry when you can't get it to work, but a kindly neighborhood teenager gets it up and running, and before long you're able to use it to balance your checkbook in half an hour, a task that took ten minutes when you had only a pocket calculator, pencil, and paper.

It's a good thing that you have become computer literate because Inkbart Ogpu, one of your rivals for CEO, a nerd who sometimes seems not of this earth, is hot on the digital trail himself. Ogpu, who came by his odd name because his parents were anthropologists who commuted between several cultures, is an expert on artificial intelligence. To know him is to believe it.

Ogpu has convinced the higher-ups that computers can

handle all the company's accounting, filing, and word processing. But like many computer mavens, Ogpu goes a bit too far. He claims that not only can the machine send form letters to a select group of the company's customers, it can also compose the letters. You're delighted. Ogpu's brain synapses must be made exclusively of semiconductors, and he is about to self-destruct. Sure enough, he's glitched when his demonstration run produces:

"A bird in the hand is worth chickens before they hatch."

"An ounce of prevention is worth its weight in gold."

Here's your opportunity. In a 250-page memo filled with computer jargon, you give top management the real lowdown on high tech. Central to your plan to solve the company's data-handling problems is a clever variation on the use of CAR. You employ this acronym twenty-seven times before you let on that it stands for Computer-Assisted Retrieval. Ordinarily, this involves the use of a computer to locate and retrieve data stored on microfilm; but applying the principles of literalism, a philosophy you picked up from an article in **Reader's Digest**, you give CAR a new twist. In your version, a mail clerk working an IBM Personal Computer with his right hand and steering a Toyota with his left uses a special fast lane in the corridors of corporate headquarters to pick up and drop off microfilm stored in boxes extending from the walls.

The icing on the cake is your scheme for computerized personnel pruning. You custom-design some software that, when fed standard input/outplace statistics, will automatically calculate the shape-up/ship-out ratio for each employee. Score low on that and you don't come back, Jack.

Everyone is terribly impressed, especially the computer illiterates. But one junior vice-president is wary of converting everything to numbers. "Numbers give people a false sense of certainty," he complains. "They seem so absolute, so impossible to argue with."

"Not to worry," you reassure him. "As Bertrand Russell once wrote, 'Mathematics may be defined as the subject in which we never know what we are talking about, nor whether what we are saying is true.'" You pause for dramatic effect. "Sounds like business as usual, doesn't it?"

If you're digitally devious and plan to use the computer to conquer, turn to page 102.

If you're a digital do-gooder and haven't a hostile thought on your mind, turn to page 105.

It is often said that no man is a hero to his valet. Familiarity breeds contempt. After all, who knows the company better than the men and women who work for it? At least you don't have to worry about strife between the different ethnic, racial, and religious groups on the premises. For ultimately they're all united by hatred for their employer.

In fact, they're ripe for a union organizing campaign. You know the Brotherhood of Featherbedders and Misfits has already spotted a golden opportunity, and a few of the brother hoods have begun to hand out pledge cards in the parking lot.

The executive committee meets in emergency session and offers you the job of making the company look like a good employer in the eyes of those who **know** better. Internal PR is especially difficult, but you won't let that stop you. In all humility, you accept the assignment.

If you think that having the CEO spend a day on the production line will convince the workers that management is "just plain folks," turn to page 99.

But if you prefer to alter the workers' lean and hungry look by throwing them some scraps, turn to page 109.

No one around here seems to care what you do, positive or negative. Socking Larry has about as much effect as kicking Jell-O. This place can absorb anything.

At the gateway to middle age, your prospects for going all the way to the top are fading fast. Your dark hair is becoming flecked with gray and your youthful zeal is turning into arthritic cynicism. But just as you are about to slide onto the slippery slope of terminal inertia, fate grins broadly. The company has decided to give in to a few mad social scientists and authorize a companywide personality screening. The idea is to put advancement and job assignments on a systematic, objective basis, eliminating the flaws inherent in the subjective judgment of department heads.

You are one of the last to be interviewed. The personnel office is a very strange place. The corridor leading to the receptionist is lined with mirrors that distort your image, like those at a carnival. The walls are painted to create optical illusions, for example making one side of the hallway appear higher than the other. It reminds you of the articles you've seen in **Scientific American** that show how spatial perceptions can be manipulated. And the Muzak in the background is just as odd — wildly hysterical laughter alternating with terrible sobbing.

Only later do you discover that this is all part of a stress test. It reaches a peak when, during the stress interview, you find yourself becoming disoriented. You think the walls are closing in. The interviewer couldn't be calmer, but after a few minutes you realize that the spatial relationships in the room are changing and, in fact, the walls **are** closing in. Those social scientists are fiendishly imaginative, you muse, as you get up and run for your life.

Flinging yourself through the door, you stumble into an arenalike area where five psychologists wearing black hoods are waiting to question you. You're asked to provide a solution to the following hypothetical business problem: Your company is being investigated by the EPA for polluting a nearby stream, the IRS is questioning the deduction of the cost of a summer home for the CEO as a corporate charitable contribution, the company cafeteria has run out of peanuts, and the Chief Executive Officer is incapacitated by hiccups. You are second in command: What do you do? "Do not take life too seriously," you quote Elbert Hubbard, a philosopher of late-nineteenth-century American business. "You will never get out of it alive." And you sit back, smug in the satisfaction of knowing that you've been cool and clever under fire.

You're almost finished. The Rorschach inkblot test is a breeze — you crammed for it last night. You are momentarily thrown, however, when they hand you an in-box full of simulated mail and memos requiring snap decisions. You've never seen a deportation notice before. The test concludes with a handwriting analysis performed by a genuine Gypsy.

94

For the results of your personality test, turn to page 103.

You left quite an impression on Larry. But you know that you can't simply duke your way to the top. An aggressive yet sensitive fellow like you has to find something more subtle. You stop off at the local bookstore to peruse their "Corporate Guerrilla Manuals" section for an answer. There, among books such as **Looking Out for Number One** and **Up Your Organization**, you discover what you've been looking for.

"I" Contact: Body Language for Everybody is a masterful compendium of anatomical idioms and a step-by-step guide to the slippery syntax of silentspeak. From now on, when at a loss for words, you won't even try to find them. Your crossed legs and folded arms will say it all. With a little effort, your reading comprehension will match your ability to "speak" the unspoken. You feel a heady sense of power. In a dog-eat-dog world, you've found a way to get a leg up on the competition.

The chapter headings in **"I" Contact** are a revelation:

95

Three Ways to Spot a Two-Faced Person in One Minute
How to Fathom a Furtive Look
Filling In the Blank Stare
Negative Feedback: How to Say No With Your Mouth Full
Backhanded Compliments and Other Nonverbal De-
    viousness
How to Curse with Your Feet
How to make Eye Contact When You're Both Wearing
    One-Way Sunglasses

Henceforth you will know yourself and other people's selves. Your fingers will do the talking and you will listen with your eyes. You will read furrowed eyebrows like tea leaves and speak volumes with a flick of the wrist, the bat of an eyelash, the twitch of an ear. You will plant seeds of doubt in the pregnant pause of a conversation, cloud people's minds with a gesture while you discern their most intimate thoughts.

Holy mackerel, this is heavy stuff!

If you think you're fluent enough in body language to have a little "talk" with the CEO, turn to page 97.

If prudence suggests that a longer period of body building is called for before you go toe to toe with the big boys, turn to page 48.

You're only a little nervous as you enter the wood-paneled office of Charles Evans Osgood, the CEO you'd like to replace. You requested an audience to offer some suggestions about running the company, knowing full well his reputation for eating alive young upstart junior executives. Forearmed is forewarned, they say, but you are more than forearmed. You are foreheaded, eyebrowed, up to your ears, and knee deep in a lethal weapon: body language.

As you reach out to shake hands, you cross your eyes and partially stick out your tongue. Osgood shudders slightly and lists to the right. "Glad to meet you," you say as you hook your left thumb into your lapel and watch his complexion turn pale. As you both sit, he starts to cross his legs, but spotting that, you counter quickly with a right-handed tug on your left earlobe. Osgood sinks back in his seat, not knowing what's happening to him. Now that you have him off balance, it is a simple matter to dispatch him.

The conversation is about time-saving techniques, but the subliminal talk is of dominance and submission. You fake him out of his chair with a hand to your own chin, and bring him to his knees with a batted eyelash. As he lifts his head to expose his throat, a submissive gesture humans have learned from wolves, you have him sign a resignation letter requesting that the board of directors appoint you CEO. You have made it all the way to the top — and you barely had to lift a finger.

The End

The coffee is hot, and so are the stock market tips from Herman the counterman. Don't sell him short; he knows what he's talking about. Herman learned about the two most important things in life — sex and stocks — on the street. Fortunately, he lived on the right street.

You and Sam put aside your business deal to deal a little for yourselves. Since you are both amateurs at the stock market, Herman explains: "It is a common misconception that a preferred stock is preferable to a common stock; common sense, however, suggests that the common is preferable to the preferred."

Today Herman is pushing an unbelievably undervalued, under-the-counter issue. He offers you both a chance to get in on the ground floor.

If you urge Sam to push the "up" button on the elevator to wealth, turn to page 107.

But if you think that Herman may be unabashedly underhanded and that you are even more likely to lose your shirt here than at the local laundry, turn to page 106.

Charles Evans Osgood hasn't gotten his hands dirty since the last time he played in a sandbox. The strongest cussword he ever uses is "bloody," he wouldn't know a boilermaker from a steam fitter, and he thinks that blue collar is a more serious form of ring around the collar. The man is such an egalitarian that he had a special side entrance built at corporate head-quarters so he could come and go without rubbing elbows with the rest of the world. He is definitely not one of the boys. But as much as he'd like to let them eat cake, he is consumed by an apoplectic hatred of unions. So he's willing to give your idea a try.

Osgood should have stayed in bed, however. He wastes half the morning in a futile search for a left-handed monkey wrench, having fallen for the oldest trick in the book. The quail quiche and Dom Perignon he produces from his lunch-box do not go over well with his fellow workers, nor do his attempts to make conversation about the relative merits of various types of polo ponies.

By late afternoon the workers have had enough. They throw a bag over Osgood's head and actually tar and feather him. You're lucky he doesn't have **you** drawn and quartered. At this point you couldn't get a job doing PR for Albert Schweitzer.

The End

The next day you get a note from the boss:

"You seem to have confused morale with chorale. This is not some kind of wacky glee club; nor is it the Boy Scouts or Camp Cucamonga. This is a business. We expect gentlemen to wear ties, ladies to wear prim business suits, and both to conduct themselves with reserve and exhibit a proper attitude. You are not supposed to be comfortable and feel good here; you are supposed to be **working**."

Just to make sure you get the point, he has made you a gift of a watch. Mickey's big hand is on the twelve and his small hand on the four. Time has certainly flown today, and with it has gone any chance that you will ever be CEO.

The End

You have fond memories of your days in Junior Achievement, the organization where kids pretend they're captains of industry. It didn't teach you any more about the business world than a good game of Monopoly, but it did allow you to begin the arduous task of making business contacts — a fine opportunity for a thirteen-year-old. Junior Government Week is based on similar principles. Corporations sponsor convocations of young, aspiring pols so that they can learn the ins and outs of our democratic way of life.

The kids brought to City Hall by your company are a spiffy-looking bunch the first morning, but by lunch hour they're beginning to play their roles too well. Some of them already have cigars dangling from their lips. By the end of the first day an eleven-year-old is ejected for trying to get a kickback on a sewer contract.

By the end of the week the press is crying for an investigation. You're in big trouble. There's talk of your being charged with corrupting the morals of a minor and some sentiment for a boycott of your company's products. You're forced to issue a public apology and your resignation is a foregone conclusion. The only ray of light is that one of the kids asks for your résumé — he's already planning his administration and will need a slick press secretary to promote his image.

The End

The difference between you and the computer illiterates around you is that you know the machine is just a tool, while they alternately fear and worship it. The people in Marketing, for example, assume that the computer will allow them to plan foolproof product campaigns. In fact, given the way the fools use the computer, they're likely to accomplish no more than the discovery that two out of every three people they interview in their surveys constitute two-thirds of their sample.

You write some key programs for the company in LISP, a pithy computer language nowhere near as well known as the ubiquitous COBOL. Every time someone demonstrates some intelligent curiosity about how any of this works, you snow them under with a blizzard of computer gobbledygook. "Why, you just call up the menu on the mainframe and retrieve modem bytes before the bit hits the fan," you remark with a wink to all questions. "You just stick it interface."

Knowledge is power; exclusive knowledge, in the Information Age, is absolute power. Finally there comes a day when the operation of the company depends completely on the operation of its computers, which depends, in turn, on **your** goodwill. That's the day you call in sick and tell them that you'll be back when they make you CEO. They have no choice. The cushy, high-backed chair is yours. Just a little solid-state statesmanship.

The End

It was the handwriting sample that gave you away. There were no discernible characteristics in your script. You are one of those rare individuals to manifest cipher syndrome: nothing is revealed in your writing. A glance behind your façade indicates that there is no you there. In fact, you **have** no personality to be tested.

You're crushed. You feel empty inside. According to them, you **are** empty inside. You have to drag yourself through the rest of the week. Friday morning you begin to clean out your desk. But just as you start to pack the framed photo of your cocker spaniel, you are summoned to the main conference room. Something must be up. They have the sterling silver and English china out and the table is spread with canapés.

At least a half dozen people pump your arm in congratulation before a member of the board of directors takes you aside and explains what's going on. With rapid changes in technology, the company needs a CEO flexible enough to bend with the breeze. You have neither roots nor personality rigidities; you are tied down to nothing. If necessary, you will let the breeze blow you all over the place, and are thus the perfect candidate. You start Monday.

The End

You should have read the graffito on the washroom wall the last time you made a pit stop: "It is better to keypunch than to be keypunched." You're about to find out just how democratic the machines really are. All things being equal, they treat everyone like a hole on an IBM card.

When you least expect it, your number comes up. One of your enemies has run your statistics through the machine, producing an appalling shape-up/ship-out ratio. You go directly from input to offkissed. You have been thoroughly digitaled — shafted the modern way.

The End

You're about as financially astute as Bozo the Clown. While you and Sam remain on the ground floor, the price of that stock goes through the roof.

Sam calls to tell you that you can forget all about that big order. He also calls your boss and tells him you're a loser.

You're as likely to become CEO as you are to become pope. You'll be lucky if the company keeps you on to lick stamps.

The End

You're a financial genius! The stock splits like rabbits fed nothing but Spanish fly. You and Sam become millionaires. In gratitude he offers you a blank order form — just fill in the numbers. Your company is so impressed with your brilliance that it announces a year before the retirement of the current CEO that you will succeed him.

But now that you've got everything you ever thought you needed, who needs it? Most of the fun was in the hunt. **Becoming** CEO was one thing; **being** CEO is something else entirely.

You put your money into a condo — a little grass shack in Hawaii. Surrounded by palm trees, pineapples, and a cockatoo or two, you while away the hours strumming on your ukulele, secure in the knowledge that you bet right all along. You'd be willing to lei odds on it.

The End

John D. Rockefeller started corporate philanthropy when he handed out dimes to children. "Hold the coin up to your ear, my child," the kindly old man would say. "What do you hear? Yes, it certainly does talk." He did yeoman service in educating a generation of young Americans to the value — and companionship — of money.

These days, of course, corporate giving is more sophisticated. While the average top-management team would prefer to endow a golf course, they can usually be prevailed upon to trust good advice and rise above their limitations. Eastern Airlines, for example, once gave a small fortune to finance a Metropolitan Opera production of Wagner's Ring cycle. It took a real act of faith to hand over their stockholders' money to pay for a bunch of fat men and women to run around in circles while they screamed their lungs out.

So which will it be? Calculated generosity to uplift Western civilization with an aesthetic boost? Or a little skinflint maneuvering to buy goodwill on a budget?

If the image committee appeals to your patronizing instincts and convinces you that the company should spend big bucks to support art, turn to page 116.

But if your idea of culture is the helpful bacteria found in a container of yogurt and you're inclined to update Rockefeller's act, turn to page 115.

The company's employees have seen the underside of the iron heel; now they're about to gaze upon the face of sweetness and light. There's nothing like the threat of a union to turn a bunch of robber barons into industrial statesmen.

You see to it that at long last the blue-collar workers get indoor plumbing (the in-house outhouse was way overdue). And the workers won't have to stay late on Christmas Eve. The company was only kidding about **that**. And when the traditional holiday birds are distributed, the plant looks like a vast turkey farm, and thus embodies what many insist is the essential spirit of the place.

But despite these humane gestures and the newsletter from top management that begins: "Dear Friends, We are workers just like you . . . ," the union continues to gather support. The executive committee overseeing your propaganda campaign suggests that you set up a "managed grapevine" to spread the word downward to the workers about the evils of unionism. Of course they believe that that grapevine will also spread the word up to you about which communist scum are supporting the union and which fine Americans favor the company.

If you agree to think "fink" and seek concord through the grapevine, turn to page 111.

If even you wouldn't do anything so shady, turn to page 110.

Top management isn't pleased with your attitude. The only kind of conscience you're expected to have is a business conscience, one flexible enough to stretch a little. Consequently they demote you to brochure writer in the PR department.

But now you're eligible to join the union, which has just won its organizing election. Your thoughts move quickly from CEO to "Solidarity Forever." Within weeks you're elected shop steward in PR.

In union there is strength — also opportunity. Five years later you've made it to president of your local. As such, you find yourself belonging to the same clubs and playing the same golf courses as top management.

Finally you become president of the International Brotherhood of Featherbedders and Misfits. You're invited to dinner at the White House, just like top management. Then it finally sinks in: You **are** top management. You're just the other side of the same coin, CEO after all.

The End

Whose idea was this? As a communications network, this grapevine is the pits. The company toadies who volunteer to spy are too stupid to convey any useful intelligence concerning support for the union down in the ranks. Nor are they capable of getting management messages for the workers straight.

When the union wins its election, you try to convince top management that it's all for the best. Now management-worker relations will be put on a more systematic basis. But the old guard won't hear of it. They think that the grapevine you cultivated produced some very sour grapes. As far as they're concerned, you're the dregs.

The End

You've come to Louie's to replenish your wardrobe from his semiannual corporate uniform sale — a package deal including pin-striped suit, Oxford shirt with discreet monogram, rep tie, wing-tipped shoes, and beige trenchcoat. For one week only he's throwing in an attaché case. Realizing that the slimmer the case, the more powerful the executive, he's chosen a beautiful cowhide leather handle attached to nothing at all.

Your problem is that a voice from within you tells you it **all** may be attached to nothing — a façade fronting a pointless game.

You consider taking the countercyclical route popularized in **Mess for Success**, the best seller that advocates pink shirts, string ties, and Mohawk haircuts. The idea is for you to become a stye in the corporate eye, like the irritant in an oyster that eventually produces a pearl.

You give it more thought. Why stop there? Why not go whole hog, heed the call of the wild, and trade in the critical-path method, cost accounting, and stock options for drugs, sex, and rock 'n' roll?

You do it. You move to Big Sur and open a health-food restaurant called Whole Grain, Wild Berries, and Nuts to You. You're your own CEO, lording it over the chef, who can produce 1,001 different tofu dishes, none of them appetizing. You're poor and going nowhere, but you're happy.

The End

The more successful you become, the clearer it is to you that Finance and Accounting will never allow you to develop your full talents. Surreptitiously, on evenings, weekends, and coffee breaks, you go to medical school, serve an internship, and by the time you're fifty, become a psychiatrist. Then you quit the company and hang out your shingle.

Before long your burgeoning psychiatry business grows into a group practice and you purchase a professional building. Soon you have to set up a separate accounting department. You acquire other group practices and open branches in all major cities. You begin to sell drive-in franchises. As a hedge against the public's losing interest in therapy, you put some of your profits into diversification, purchasing a potato chip manufacturer and a casket company.

Of course, you have long since given up your own practice — too much time is required to run this empire. One day, while admiring your hand-tailored suit in the mirror, it hits you: You're a CEO after all.

The End

114

With Christmas just past, you hire several thousand laid-off Santa Clauses dirt cheap to work the streets giving out tokens to kids on behalf of your company. The tokens, the size of a dime, are worth a dollar apiece toward the purchase of company products, but they may not be used for at least two months and they're not transferable. In fact, a tiny notice that your company places among the lost-and-found ads in the papers specifies that the kids may use the tokens to purchase only shaving cream or chewing tobacco.

Yes, you know how mean that is, but the important thing is that the media have already given you coverage. The TV lights have been turned off, the image of a kind and benevolent company has been created. That image is real. Real reality is imaginary.

Over the years you perpetrate more dirty tricks and your reputation as a PR genius grows like a landfill. At sixty you're chosen CEO. You're a nasty old man who willfully cheats widows and orphans, a miscreant who's built a career on making misanthropy look like philanthropy. A Scrooge you are, and a Scrooge you shall remain.

The End

Al Capp, whose contribution to art was "Li'l Abner," once said of abstract art that it was "a product of the untalented, sold by the unprincipled to the utterly bewildered." While you prefer realism, you have to admit that you'd feel quite comfortable in the art world Capp describes.

But it's the art of black magic that interests you most. You need to conjure up an image of a public-spirited company. And while creating that image, you must keep an eye on your colleagues, whose own favorite image would be that of themselves as CEO.

Lila LaBelle is a particular problem. She's an art major who spent a year at the Sorbonne and graduated from Sarah Lawrence. When in college, LaBelle was a participant in the company's take-a-hippie-to-lunch program, aimed at rehabilitating disaffected youth. Now that she's finally shed her sandals for sensible shoes, you detect the glint of ambition in her eye. Despite her amateur standing, she could be dangerous.

"Here's our chance to pioneer on the frontiers of aesthetics," LaBelle opines. "We could revolutionize corporate giving by issuing no-strings-attached grants to unaffiliated avantegarde artists."

"Take it easy," you admonish her. "We don't want to get carried away. Remember, we don't want to **do** good, just look good. I'm inclined to think that we should be hiring a hack to cover a couple of canvases with safe subjects — you know, sunsets, moonbeams, stardust, sweet dreams."

But LaBelle is adamant, and she has the committee behind her. You finally compromise on a tile mural depicting some theme of social significance, to be applied to the lobby wall of corporate headquarters. You know that there's a quick way to cut your losses should the artist do something offensive. RCA hired Diego Rivera to do a similar work for them in the 1930s. When he had the gall to put an image of Lenin in the mural, the company paid him off and then had the whole thing chipped away. There are any number of chiselers in your company who could quickly do the same if it came down to it.

You see the work just before its unveiling — and you're immensely pleased. It's a panorama of daily life in ancient Egypt. What were you worrying about? In fact, you like it enough to see to it that LaBelle and the rest of them get no credit. You and you alone will be the company's patronizer of the arts.

But you should have read the fine print. An amateur Egyptologist at the official unveiling reads aloud from the hieroglyphics at the edge of the work. It's full of references to sexual perversions and subversive political ideas. You'll be old and gray before you finish removing the mural with the penknife they gave you. You will not be CEO. You will not even make it to head janitor.

The End

"Comptroller" definitely turns out to be the wrong choice. It has a less natural sound, and selecting it has identified you as an eccentric. Your "assignment," in reality, was a secret personality test to ferret out potential troublemakers.

You're directed to report to the outplacement desk, where you're asked to turn in your company keychain and tie clip. When you try to argue, the woman manning the desk suggests that you go back to Russia, where you probably came from.

The End

A change of scene is what you need, but you're not up to mastering a new corporate culture. Unable to sustain your current pace, and realizing that your listening post is getting you no closer to CEO, you close up shop and fade back into the corporate woodwork, content to oversee the balancing of balance sheets and the stating of income statements.

The years pass. Osgood is getting no younger, but that means little to you. He seems like a distant figure who no longer has any connection to your life.

One day death comes to old Osgood, as it must to all of us. Barely has he departed this vale of tears when the board of directors convenes to pick his successor.

"Should I be called," observes Snodgrass in one of his noble postures, "I will serve selflessly, manage magnanimously, and rule with rectitude."

"Should you be 'called,'" you mutter under your breath, "I will eat a telex machine."

Then word gets out that the directors seek a manager for the times: someone bland, unassertive, easily manipulated, without genuine charisma, a little on the dull side. He should be affable, but not a good-time Charlie. They are looking for someone with gray hair and an even grayer personality.

Given those criteria, the identity of the new CEO is a foregone conclusion. Do telex machines come in chocolate?

The End